MY PET
SPIDER

Michelle Lomberg

Weigl Publishers Inc.

Published by Weigl Publishers Inc.
350 5th Avenue, Suite 3304 PMB 6G
New York, NY 10118-0069
Website: www.weigl.com

Project Coordinator
Heather C. Hudak

Design and Layout
Terry Paulhus

Library of Congress Cataloging-in-Publication Data available upon request.
Fax 1-866-44-WEIGL for the attention of the Publishing Records department.

ISBN 978-1-60596-094-4 (hard cover)
ISBN 978-1-60596-095-1 (soft cover)

Printed in China
1 2 3 4 5 6 7 8 9 0   13 12 11 10 09

Photograph and Text Credits

Weigl acknowledges Getty Images as its primary image supplier for this title.

Rick C. West: Page 23 top; Photofest: Page 26.

Every reasonable effort has been made to trace ownership and to obtain permission to reprint copyright
material. The publishers would be pleased to have any errors or omissions brought to their attention so that
they may be corrected in subsequent printings.

All of the Internet URLs given in the book were valid at the time of publication.
However, due to the dynamic nature of the Internet, some addresses may have
changed, or sites may have ceased to exist since publication. While the author
and publisher regret any inconvenience this may cause readers, no responsibility
for any such changes can be accepted by either the author or the publisher.

Contents

Eight-legged Friends

Spiders have a bad reputation. Many people are terrified of these eight-legged creatures, but the truth is that very few spiders are dangerous to humans. Most spiders are shy, gentle creatures that make interesting, unusual pets. Pet spiders are very easy to care for. They are able to live in a small space. They do not need to be brushed or walked, and they do not need to be fed daily.

All spiders have fangs that eject **venom**. Not all venom is dangerous to humans.

Even though spiders do not need much attention, they are still a big responsibility. A spider's enclosure must be kept at the right temperature and **humidity**. It must also be kept clean. Spiders need to eat live food, such as crickets and moths. They also require care if they are sick or injured.

Spiders are not like cats or dogs. They spend most of the day hiding and should not be handled often. Spider owners must be very patient. Patience will be rewarded with a glimpse into the lives of these unusual creatures.

Spider Specs

- There are more than 35,000 **species** of spiders. About 3,000 live in North America.
- All spiders make silk, but not all spiders spin webs.
- The fear of spiders is called arachnophobia.

- The largest spider is the goliath bird-eating tarantula. His leg span can reach 10 inches (25 centimeters) in **diameter**.

Pet Profiles

Spiders come in many sizes and colors. Most spiders are calm, gentle, and shy. Others are aggressive and may give a painful bite. Only experienced spider owners should keep aggressive or dangerous spiders as pets. Tarantulas are the largest and most common pet spiders. There are more than 800 species of tarantula. Other spiders kept as pets include giant orb weavers, widows, and wolf spiders. Common house and garden spiders also make enjoyable pets. Most spiders are terrestrial or arboreal. Terrestrial spiders live in burrows in the ground. Arboreal spiders live in trees.

Mexican Redknee Tarantula

- Black in color with orange bands on leg joints
- Grows to about 5 inches (13 cm) across
- Females can live up to 20 years
- Lives in a range of temperatures
- Terrestrial
- Calm **temperament**

Pinktoe Tarantula

- Dark in color with pink or red patches on the ends of its legs
- Females can live 8 or 9 years
- Calm temperament, but can be easily startled
- Spends most of her time hiding in her web
- Arboreal

6

CHILEAN ROSE TARANTULA

- Tan, pink, or red in color
- Grows to about 4 inches (10 cm) across
- Calm temperament, but may bite if handled
- One of the most common breeds for new spider owners to raise
- Terrestrial

FALSE WIDOW SPIDER

- Dark in color with yellow, white, or red markings
- Smaller than 1 inch (2.5 cm) across
- Weak venom makes them less dangerous than the black widow spider
- Calm temperament
- Requires little care
- Arboreal

CAROLINA WOLF SPIDER

- Gray-brown in color with gray hair
- Adult females grow to 4 inches (10 cm) across
- Females can live 3 years; males live 1.5 years
- Should not be handled
- Requires little care
- Terrestrial

GOLDEN SILK ORB WEAVER

- Gray-brown in color, with golden brown markings
- Grows to 5 inches (13 cm) across
- Weaves large, golden webs
- Needs a large living space
- Calm temperament
- Arboreal

Spider History

Spiders have lived on Earth for about 400 million years. This history has been difficult to study because spider **fossils** are difficult to find. Spider fossils are rare because spiders have soft bodies with no bones. A few ancient spiders have been preserved in **amber**. Others have left impressions in soft rock. Using this information, scientists have been able to trace the history of spiders.

In the U.S., fewer than five people die from spider bites each year.

Spiders are arthropods. *Arthropod* is a Greek word that means "jointed feet." Insects and shellfish, such as crabs and lobsters, are arthropods, too. Arthropods are descendants of ancient worms called Annelida. These were similar to modern earthworms.

Spiders belong to a special class of arthropods that are called arachnids. The arachnid group also includes mites, ticks, and scorpions. The very first arachnids lived in the water about 450 million years ago. They looked like scorpions. The earliest land arachnids were Trigonotarbids, or trigs. Trigs looked like tiny spiders, but they did not have fangs or **spinnerets**.

The first modern spider lived about 380 million years ago. Even though spiders have lived with humans for thousands of years, it was not until the 1970s that they became popular pets.

Web Weavers

- The nursery rhyme character Little Miss Muffet was a real girl. Her father believed that eating spiders would cure the common cold.
- Spiders have no bones.

- Spider webs have been used as folk remedies to cure warts and to stop bleeding.

Life Cycle

The life span of spiders depends on the species. Many smaller spiders live only one year. Some tarantulas live more than 20 years. In all species, females live longer than males.

Eggs

Spiders begin life as eggs. The female spider spins a special web called an egg sac to hold her eggs. Some spiders carry the sac with them, and others hide it. Eggs take a few weeks to a few months to hatch, depending on the species and the temperature.

Hatchlings

Most hatchlings are born hairless, colorless, and without claws. They cannot eat. Hatchlings remain in the egg sac until they shed their outer skin and grow a new one.

Spiderlings

Once spiderlings have shed their first skin, they begin to eat. Their first meal is usually an unhatched egg or a weaker sibling. Most spiderlings must fend for themselves. For some species, the mother cares for her babies. She protects them and brings them food until they are able to look after themselves. The wolf spider carries her babies on her back until they are one week old. Other spiderlings spin a strand of silk that allows them to be carried off by the wind.

Mature Spiders

Spiders have soft bodies that are covered in a hard exoskeleton. The exoskeleton is an outer skin that cannot grow. Spiders must shed the exoskeleton when they have outgrown it. This process is called molting. Most spiders molt once in a while until they are adults. Mature female tarantulas continue to molt once or twice each year.

living life

- Some spiders lay only a few eggs. Others lay as many as 2,000.
- The eggs of some large spiders are the size of green peas.
- Some tarantulas can take as long as 10 years to mature.

Picking Your Pet

If you think you need to be fearless to own a spider, think again. Spiders are timid, fragile animals. They need an owner who will be patient and gentle. Consider the following questions before choosing your pet.

Always keep your spider's cage at the proper humidity. If your spider's exoskeleton becomes too dry, he may have trouble molting.

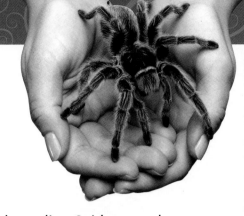

What Will a Spider Cost?

The best place to buy a spider is from a **reputable** pet store or **breeder**. The cost of your spider will depend on the species. Rare spiders are more expensive. When calculating the cost of buying a pet spider, be sure to include the cost of food, an enclosure, and supplies. Spiders need to eat live food, such as crickets, mealworms, or baby mice. Spiders do not need to make regular visits to a **veterinarian**. They rarely require medical treatment, and they do not need to be **vaccinated**.

How Should I Choose My Spider?

Choose a spider that has been bred in **captivity**. Spiders captured in nature are in danger of one day becoming **extinct**.

How Will Owning a Spider Affect My Family?

Many people are afraid of spiders. Before bringing a spider home, find out if members of your family are afraid of them. Try to educate your family about spiders using books, television programs, videos, and websites. If the thought of sharing a home with a spider still scares family members, you should consider a different pet.

If any member of your household has a history of allergies, you should not get a spider. Very few spiders have venom that can kill a person. However, even weak venom can cause an allergic reaction. Even if you are not allergic to spiders, tarantula hairs can produce a terrible rash.

fascinating fangs

- The Australian funnel web spider can pierce bone with its fangs.
- No two spider webs are the same.

- The female golden silk orb weaver is about 1 inch (2.5 cm) across. The male golden silk orb weaver is only 0.125 inch (0.3 cm) across.

Spider Supplies

Your spider will need to live in an enclosure. The type of enclosure depends on the type of spider. Is he terrestrial or arboreal? Does he thrive in a dry or humid climate? Learn as much as you can about your spider in order to provide the most suitable enclosure.

If your spider's enclosure is too dry, use a spray bottle to sprinkle a fine mist. Do not spray the spider directly.

Most spiders should live alone. If two or more spiders are housed together, they may kill and eat each other. Your spider's enclosure should be about twice as wide as his leg span, and about three times as long. If you have a

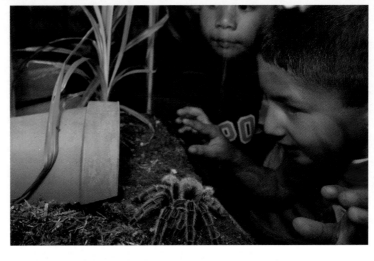

burrowing spider, the top of the enclosure should not be too high. Falling from a height of just 6 inches (15 cm) can kill a spider. Arboreal spiders need larger, taller enclosures than terrestrial spiders.

Plastic boxes with snap-on lids are ideal for terrestrial spiders. Be sure to punch several small holes into the lid to let air in. Glass fish tanks can also make a suitable home for some spiders. The tank should have a secure lid.

The spider's enclosure will need a **substrate**. For burrowing spiders, this should be a mixture of sand, peat moss, bark chips, and vermiculite, or minerals that absorb water. The type of mixture depends on how much humidity your spider needs. Pine and cedar bark are **toxic** to spiders and should not be used. Arboreal spiders will need some branches on which to build their webs.

If you remove food **carcasses** regularly, you should only have to clean out your spider's enclosure twice a year. Use a long pair of tweezers to remove food carcasses.

Spider Spaces

- Some spiders are communal, which means they live in large groups. A communal web can hold as many as 20,000 spiders.

- Water spiders live underwater. They build bell-shaped webs and fill them with air bubbles.

Feeding Your Spider

All spiders are carnivores. This means they are meat-eaters. Most spiders eat insects. Some large tarantulas eat mice, lizards, and other small animals. Not all spiders use their webs to catch food. Some lie in wait for their **prey**. Others chase their meal. All spiders use their venom to stun or kill their prey.

If you catch insects or worms to feed your spider, be sure they have not been sprayed with **pesticides**.

16

Since spiders do not have teeth for chewing, they are only able to drink their food. Spiders inject their prey with digestive juices. These juices turn the prey's insides into liquid. The spider sucks this liquid and leaves the carcass behind.

Most spiders will only eat live food. Crickets are the most common food for pet spiders.

Live crickets can be purchased at a pet store. Beetles, earthworms, grasshoppers, houseflies, and moths are also good food for a spider.

It is important to remove uneaten food and carcasses from your spider's enclosure. Live prey can produce young that may attack your spider while it is molting. Leftover carcasses can grow fungus or attract **parasites** that are dangerous to your spider.

Spiders need fresh water. Provide clean water in a shallow dish. Place a piece of sponge inside the water dish. If your spider falls in the water, she can climb out using the sponge. Replace the sponge regularly so that it does not grow mold.

feeding frenzy

- It takes a tarantula one to two days to digest a mouse.
- The bola spider throws a sticky ball of silk at her prey.

Spider Parts

With their hard exoskeletons and quick movements, spiders have much in common with ants and beetles. However, spiders are not insects. There are several differences between spiders and insects. Insects have six legs and three main body parts. Spiders have eight legs and two main body parts.

A spider uses his fangs to poison his prey with venom. Using his fangs, he injects prey with digestive juices. Most spiders' fangs point toward one another. Tarantula fangs point straight down.

A spider's silk comes out of his spinnerets. Spiders spin different kinds of silk for different purposes.

The front part of a spider's body is called the cephalothorax. This term combines the Greek words for "head" and "chest." The hard shell of the cephalothorax is called the carapace.

A spider breathes through slits in his abdomen. His lungs are called book lungs because they look like the pages of a book. Book lungs are not very efficient. A spider cannot run far before he must stop to catch his breath.

Like all arthropods, a spider has an exoskeleton. This tough shell protects the soft body inside.

All spiders have eight legs. Spiders taste and smell through organs in their legs.

Most spiders have eight eyes—two large ones and six smaller ones. Most spiders do not see very well.

Pedipalps are used like human hands. Spiders use their pedipalps for holding food.

Handling Your Spider

Handling a spider is always risky. Spiders do not enjoy being handled. All spiders can bite. A spider's bite can be very harmful to a human.

To prevent injury to your pet, never pick up your spider by her abdomen.

If a spider is accidentally dropped, she can be seriously injured or killed. To prevent your spider from being injured, she should be handled as little as possible.

If you must remove a spider from her enclosure, it is safest to use a container. Place the opening of a jar or plastic container in front of your spider. Using a soft paintbrush, gently nudge the spider toward the container. Once the spider is inside, place the lid on the container. Make sure there are small air holes in the lid.

Body Bits

- The body of a newly-molted spider is very fragile. She cannot stand or move until her legs have hardened. Never handle a molting spider.

- Tarantulas head for higher ground when startled. They may run up a person's arm if spooked.

Healthy and Happy

Most veterinarians do not treat spiders. Still, a veterinarian who specializes in exotic pets may be able to answer questions about your spider's health.

If your spider looks shriveled and walks awkwardly, he is probably dehydrated. Make sure your spider always has fresh drinking water.

Two things that can harm a pet spider are injuries and parasites. Spiders can injure their legs if they fall, if they have trouble molting, or if they are attacked by a **predator**. A spider can survive the loss of a leg. Special muscles at the base of the leg close the wound and stop the bleeding. A new leg will grow when the spider molts. An injury to the abdomen is very serious. If the wound is small, it may be sealed with a dab of petroleum jelly.

Parasites can threaten the health of your spider. Mites and scuttle flies are the most common pests. Mites are tiny, light-colored dots that might crawl on a spider. Mites can enter a spider's lungs and make him ill. Mites can also attack the spider while he is molting. Scuttle flies lay eggs on tarantulas. When the eggs hatch, the **maggots** crawl into the spider's mouth and eat his insides. Mites and scuttle flies are attracted to the spider's uneaten food. Promptly removing waste from the enclosure can help prevent these pests from harming your spider.

Heart Smart

- Spider blood is blue.
- A spider's heart is shaped like a long tube.

Spider Behavior

A happy spider is usually an inactive spider. Most spiders are content to spend all day in their enclosure. Spiders build different kinds of shelters inside their enclosures.

A tarantula bite is said to feel like a bee sting.

Some terrestrial spiders dig burrows in the substrate. Others hide under pieces of bark or other objects. Arboreal spiders spin shelters out of silk. Most spiders are nocturnal. This means they only leave their shelters at night.

A spider will let you know when she is stressed or scared. Digging, pacing, or climbing are signs that a spider is not happy in her home. A scared or angry spider will try to look bigger by raising her abdomen. She may rear up and show her fangs. Some species even hiss when they are angry. Many tarantulas brush the hair off their abdomens when they feel threatened. These hairs, called **urticating** hairs, are a weapon. They can cause skin, eye, and throat irritation. If a spider shows any of these signs, she may be dangerous to handle.

Pet Peeves

Spiders do not like:
- being handled
- other spiders
- too much attention
- bright lights
- loud noises

Enemy Attack

- Some spiders use **camouflage** to hide from their enemies. One species, called the bird-dropping spider, disguises herself as a bird dropping.

- Natural enemies of spiders include birds, frogs, lizards, toads, and wasps.

Spider Stories

In all parts of the world, spiders have fascinated people throughout history. Perhaps the most popular American spider story is *Charlotte's Web* by E.B. White. This novel tells the story of a clever spider who writes messages in her web to save a pig's life.

Grandmother Spider Steals the Fire

The Choctaw Peoples of Tennessee and Mississippi believe the Grandmother Spider taught humans how to make and use fire. When people first came to be on Earth, their bodies were wrapped in cocoons. The Great Spirit sent someone to Earth to unwrap them and open their eyes. Since Earth was dark, their eyes saw nothing, and the air was cold. To warm their bodies and light their way, Grandmother Spider left to steal fire from people in the East. When she returned, she taught humans how to use fire. She also taught humans how to make clay pottery and weave.

Arachnids are named after Arachne, a character in Roman mythology. Arachne was very proud of her ability to weave. One day, the goddess Minerva challenged Arachne to a weaving contest. Arachne's weaving was better than that of the goddess. Minerva was furious. Arachne felt terrible that she had angered the goddess. She was so upset that she hanged herself. Minerva felt sorry for the girl. She changed Arachne into a spider so Arachne could continue weaving.

American Indians have great respect for spiders. In Hopi mythology, the Spider Woman helped create life on Earth. Using dirt and saliva, she created a pair of twins. One twin formed the new Earth into solid ground. The other gave the world its sounds and echoes.

Today, spiders appear in books and movies. The Spider-Man comic book series was created in the 1960s. The story is about a boy named Peter Parker who becomes a superhero after he is bitten by a spider. The comic book was made into a television cartoon series and a movie.

Story Spiders

- The people of Taranto, Italy, once believed that a spider bite could only be cured by performing a lively dance called the tarantella.

- Spiders appear in the mythology of people from ancient Rome, Africa, and North America.

Pet Puzzlers

What do you know about spiders? If you can answer the following questions correctly, you may be ready to own a pet spider.

Q How can I tell if my spider is angry?

A An angry spider might rear up, bare his fangs, and raise his abdomen. Some species hiss when they are angry.

Q Should you decorate your spider's enclosure with pine and cedar bark?

A No. Pine and cedar are toxic to spiders.

Q What is the difference between a terrestrial spider and an arboreal spider?

A A terrestrial spider lives on the ground. An arboreal spider lives in a tree.

Q Is it a good idea to keep two spiders in the same enclosure?

A It is not a good idea to keep two spiders in the same enclosure. Sometimes, spiders fight or even kill one another.

Q Why should you buy a spider bred in captivity?

A Spiders caught in nature are in danger of becoming extinct. Captive breeding helps protect spiders in their natural habitats.

Q Do spiders chew their food?

A No. Spiders drink their food. They use digestive juices to turn their prey to liquid.

Q Why do spiders molt?

A Spiders molt because their hard exoskeletons cannot grow. When a spider gets too big for his skin, he must molt.

Calling Your Spider

Before you buy your pet spider, write down some spider names you like. Some names may work better for a female spider. Others may suit a male spider. Here are just a few suggestions.

Boris

Charlotte

Spidey

Spinner

Fang

Webster

Hairy

Itsy-Bitsy

Octavia

Frequently Asked Questions

Should I put toys or decorations in my spider's enclosure?

Spiders do not need to play. If you want to decorate your spider's enclosure, make sure you do not use anything that can fall or roll on top of your spider. House plants make a nice addition to a spider's enclosure. Plants also keep the air humid. Small pots can be secured in the substrate.

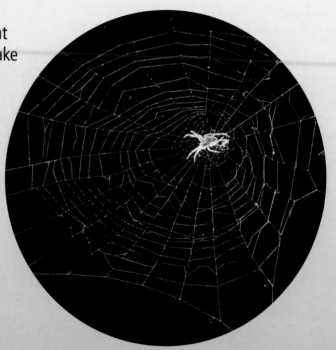

If my spider is lying on his back, is he dead?

Spiders lie on their backs to molt. Dead spiders usually lie on their bellies with their legs curled underneath.

Is it legal to own a spider?

Some states have passed laws banning people from keeping certain species of spiders as pets. If you buy your spider from a reputable pet store or breeder, she is probably legal. Still, it is a good idea to check the state and local laws before you buy a spider.

More Information

Animal Organizations

You can help spiders stay healthy and happy by learning more about them. Many organizations are dedicated to teaching people how to care for and protect their pet pals. For more spider information, write to the following organizations.

Australian Tarantula Association

27 Saunders Bay Rd
Caringbah, Sydney NSW
AUSTRALIA
2229

International Society of Arachnology

Museum f. Naturkunde
Humboldt Univ. zu Berlin
Invalidenstrasse 43
Berlin 10115, Germany

Websites

To answer more of your spider questions, go online, and surf to the following websites.

American Arachnological Society

www.americanarachnology.org

American Tarantula Society

www.atshq.org

Tarantula Guide

www.tarantulaguide.com

Words to Know

amber: the hardened sap of ancient trees

breeder: a person who raises specific types of animals or plants

camouflage: special coloring that allows animals to hide

captivity: the state of being kept or owned

carcasses: dead bodies

diameter: the measurement of a straight line passing through the center of a circle

extinct: no longer living anywhere on Earth

fossils: rocklike remains of ancient animals or plants

humidity: moisture

maggots: worms hatched from the eggs of flies

parasites: animals or plants that feed off another animal or plant

pesticides: chemicals that kill insects and spiders

predator: an animal that hunts for food

prey: an animal that is hunted for food

reputable: known to be honest and fair

species: a group of similar plants or animals

spinnerets: the organs with which a spider spins silk

substrate: the bottom layer of a spider's enclosure

temperament: personality

toxic: poisonous

urticating: stinging or irritating; may cause a rash

vaccinated: to protect from a disease

venom: a poisonous liquid some animals use to cause harm to predators and prey

veterinarian: animal doctor

Index